Children's Author
Presentation
Handbook

Written and compiled by Georgette Baker and Ramona Moreno Winner.
bakergeorgette@yahoo.com
Ramona@brainstorm3000.com

Ramona Moreno Winner & Georgette Baker

TABLE OF CONTENTS

Preparing to Present Your Book

You want to present your book or learning materials (product) in a classroom, assembly or library setting.

1. What is your goal when offering to present?

2. Are you simply out to share information about your product?

3. Do you want to sell your product?

4. Do you want to get paid for presenting?

Sharing with Children

Making your book come alive to a young audience requires more than the ability to read. In our world today, children are accustomed to being stimulated visually and quickly through electronic games, videos and fast-paced television programs. This is your competition.

There is no guarantee that if you read your book in your normal voice, with no preparation, that you will have a captive audience. No matter how good your story is, it will come across as mundane and boring if you are not a good presenter.

Here is what we recommend you do:

Record your storytelling. Videotape it. Upon reviewing the video, did you find yourself interesting? Listen to your voice. Is it animated? Remember who your competition is and modify your presentation. The internet makes that possible.

Not every author will be able to be a great presenter without practice, so practice! Rehearse your presentation in front of a mirror, in front of family, or in front for friends.

Determine if it is really necessary to read the whole book during a presentation, or if you can pique your audience's interest more by reading bits of the book and sharing expereinces or activities that delve deeper into your message.

*My very first book, **It's Okay to be Different!** had a wonderful*

message, but it was too long for the age group for which it was

intended. The illustrations were bright and playful, so I ended

up reading the first page, thumbing through the book to illus-

trate examples of being the same and different, and closing

with the reading of the last page which celebrated each child

for his/her unique qualities. I followed up my presentation

with an activity. Each child smelled candles scented the same

and found that they detected different fragrances. (R)

Find what your competition is dong that makes them successful. In your presentation; incorporate some of your competitor's "tricks." You want children to be engaged in your delivery. If you are boring, you-cannot expect children to want to buy your book.

During your presentation, children may become unruly; they may talk among them-selves or start playing together.

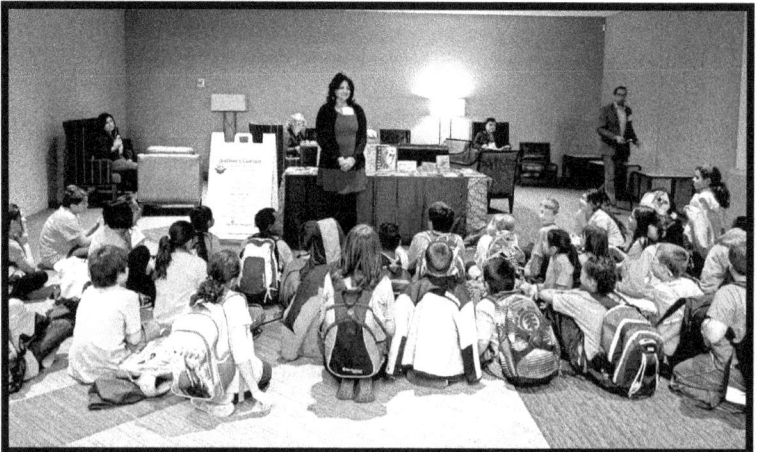

They are not being deliberately rude, they are just not captivated by your delivery.

L earn to request a separation of grades or ages appropriate to your presentation. A presentation for a K-2 group should have different material than a presentation for K-5, 6-8, or 9-12 grades. Learn your market and understand it. If you have never been around large groups of children, you have much to learn.

Using Storytelling to Present Your Book

As an instructor of advanced storytelling, I often tell my students and teachers that if you visualize what your character is feeling, then you have a greater opportunity of conveying that feeling. If the character in your book is happy, you need to remember that feeling. If the character is afraid, you need to dig down deep to remember a time when you were afraid and use that experience to tell that part of your story. In one of my stories, a little bird cries in despair. Most of us have cried. We have known situations where we were afraid. My character is lost and crying. I have been lost. I've been lost while driving and while traveling. I have lost things that were important to me, and I have cried. I use all of my past experiences and bring them into the moment as they relate to my story. My listeners are engaged and experiencing my book. (G)

U se Your Body as a Visual Aid.

There is more that can be done to embellish the story. You can move your body. If you look up and peer, the children will look up and peer.

If your character is peering into a hole as you tell your story, then you "peer into a hole." Don't just look down, but imagine that hole that you've written about. Imagine the tree, the bush, the dog, whatever it is that you want them to see. You need to see it and feel it. When you feel it, they will feel it! Use your hand to signify you are opening a window or a door. Widen your eyes if that is what your character is doing. Ask the children to do the same. Now they are participating and they are engaged. If your character is walking, have children clap (tell them how many times; it is not easy to stop them once they get going) to create the sound of walking. (G)

U se Your Voice.

Voice intonation is important too. You can raise your voice; make it squeaky, speak softly, adopt an accent, speak hurriedly or breathlessly. Whatever emotion your character is experiencing at the time, you can convey with a change of voice . You could give each of your characters a different voice; you **know** how to do that. Daily, humans mimic people. Perhaps you have mimicked someone's attitude, their manner of speaking, the sound of their voice. You are the only show in town with your book in hand, so, make it a good one. (G)

E ach author has a different personality and a different ability of story telling. Do it your way. Do it how **you** feel comfortable, but do it so it grabs the attention of your audience.

★ When you present, get someone to go with you and have them record from an iphone or pad. You may even get a nice piece you can use on your website

> *If you feel you have no talent for acting or are tone deaf like some of us claim to be, connect with a local Toastmaster group and learn how to speak in front of a group. There, you can learn how to interact with a group, use props and displays, learn about pacing and voice modulation, and rid yourself of those ah's and um's, all the while gaining confidence as a speaker. (R)*

Remember, you are presenting to children, whether grammar school or high school, the purchases come from teachers and parents, so your presentation must also be entertaining for them.

If you have a large group, a projection screen of your book is often helpful. Any opportunity to have them experience your story is good. For example, if you have a book on ants, bring a visual of an ant farm. If you decide to use visual aids, have them look professional. If you are using up-to-date technology, be sure to test your software and your computer. Make certain all your files are in order and ready for projection.

Handle all your digital needs prior to arriving at your engagement.

Sharing With Your Audience.

If you intend to share something that your audience will drink, eat, or rub on their skin, you should carry liability insurance. Make certain everyone, including teachers, parents, and administrators, understand that you will be offering samples. Do this prior to your presentation.

Small Group Presentations
vs
Large Group Presentations

In a perfect world, you will get to choose the environment you want to present in. If you call the shots, you will be able to choose to present in a classroom or an auditorium. However, things change, so flexibility is important! You may be expecting to present in a classroom and have control over the questions the children pose. Next thing you know, you are presenting in an auditorium with many classroom groups and nobody is asking you anything. Be prepared to be flexible and have a Plan B. Be ready to change what you were going to do. It is possible you do not have access to a chalkboard or a visual that all can see, as you were counting on. This is where your practice using your body to tell the story comes into play. The more flexible and prepared you are, the easier it will be to overcome any unexpected change.

If you have a large group, recruit teachers or parents to help maintain order or pass things out. Remember to never dismiss a question and always show respect, even when you are harried. Be ready for anything. That includes being outside, being with disabled children, autistic children, children older than you expected or much younger than you expected. That is what you are getting paid for.

Enjoy yourself. You love your storybook or novel. Children want to be entertained; they like stories. Share your story with joy and don't be anxious. It will be alright, you have prepared!

★ If you do better with smaller groups, then only promote your services to classroom settings

Getting Paid

Yes, we all want to be paid for what we do. However, you may need to book some "gigs" for free in order to improve your presentation skills as well as your confidence.

Have a few practice runs. Speak for free in a grade school. Make sure you videotape or audiotape yourself as well as the audience so you can see how children are reacting to your presentation. With a video of their faces, you can evaluate their reaction at each part of your book and determine:

- When did they stop listening?
- Where were they totally engaged?
- Where did they laugh?

You need to know this. Your clients may pay you once, but if you become known as a very boring presenter you will not continue to be invited to present. Of course, this may not pertain to you if your book has already sold millions of copies.

Selling Your Product at the Event

Children do not have money. They cannot buy your book unless you let thier parents know that you will be appearing at the school. Do not count on the school to advertise your visit. Make sure you have a flyer with a detachable order form.

Ensure there is a date when you will be visitng the school, who you are, what you will be presenting, and information about yourself. Example below:

Georgette Baker will be visiting Oakridge Elementary on

August 5, 2016 at 10:30 a.m.

Ms. Baker is the author of 32

bilingual books and CD's of traditional children's

music. She will be performing and telling

stories from some of her books.

To order an advanced, signed copy, fill out the form below

The detachable form should have a place for the child's name, grade, the name of his/her teacher, type of payment: check, cash, or credit card. It you have more than one book, make sure you have the titles and prices listed with little check boxes so they can check which one they want.

I once sent flyers that did not include collection of zip code for the billing address on credit cards. It was a nightmare getting hold of the card-holders and I could not collect on several of my orders. (R)

Book A: Copies _____$19.95   Book B: Copies _____$10.95

Child's Name: _____ Grade: _____

Teacher: _____ Room Number: _____

Amount of Check: _____ Cash: _____

Return this form by 8/4/2016 to Mrs. B's, room B

If you are able to book assemblies far in advance, you have an opportunity to send a poster or a digital file of a poster to whomever is arranging your visit, as well as an advance copy of your book(s). This allows students and teachers to become familiar with your work and serves to promote sales. In this case, you would also send out an order form listing your book(s) for sale.

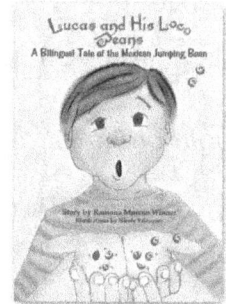

Get these flyers to the school, at the very latest, one week before you are about to present. Give your contact person the date the book orders are to be turned in, and arrange with him/her who is to be in charge of collecting them.

I give them the form up to a month prior to the event so I can preorder my books(if I don't have them in inventory). (G)

Call the person gathering the orders for you and find out how many books you need to take to the school. Meet with the person before your presentation, autograph the books to the respective child, collect your money, and put the order form into the book so that the person gathering the signed books knows where they are to go.

I like to place an "Autographed by the Author" sticker on the cover of each signed book. (R)

The school is not going to do this for you, they don't care if you sell books. You need to do the work. You need to ensure someone will collect the money. Usually the librarian or whomever booked you will help with this function. Make sure you have a few extra books for those children who will be bringing money that day. This is how you sell books when you go to present.

⭐ Donate a book to the school library.

Marketing - How do you Begin?

As an author, your job does not end with writing and publishing your book. If you want children to see it, and parents and teachers to become aware of it, your job is just beginning. If you are self-publishing, your advanced education in marketing, distribution, and public speaking is just beginning. Don't be afraid; this is your first step into that process.

Email is essential. If you have email and you have been promoting yourself, you need to check your email regularly, including your spam folder. You don't want to miss a job you worked so hard to get. Include your email address in **all** of your promotional material.

Promotional materials include business cards, as well as flyers and oversized postcards that you send out, give out, and put inside your book. When you go to print your book, you can include an order form with the titles of your other books within the back pages of your newly-printed book. Never miss an opportunity to promote yourself.

Your website should contain contact information: email address, phone number, and mailing address. You should include a biography sharing information your readers might find interesting. A synopsis of your book(s) and articles that may have been written about you or your books should be part of your web page. Don't forget to share where they can purchase your book(s) and a price list.

Newspaper articles are always great to include. It is really not difficult to get some kind of information about yourself in the newspaper. Find the name of the local editor of the entertainment section of your local newspaper and his his/her name and email address. Write your own article or news release. It is easier for newspaper reporters to edit information that is already written for them, and it increases your chance of getting into the newspaper. After you write what you want published (include when, what, where, who), email your release to the reporter with the words **Press Release** written at the top. Include your name and contact information (email address and phone). If you submit electronically, in pdf form, you can link your website or youtube clip within the text. Make sure your article has a title that will entice the reporter to read your press release.

You are submitting something unsolicited, so make it easy to use. Give an eye-catching title to spur their interest. If nothing grandiose comes to mind, then use one of these basic ones:

Local Author Writes About _____

Local Author to Speak at _____ Elementary School

Local Author to Sign Books at _____

Your local paper will be interested in you because your are **local.** If you can find something unique to tell about yourself and your book, a bigger paper can be enticed to cover your story.

I have been written up in magazines that reviewed my books and newspapers that published my stories, including the LA Times and La Opinion, countless times because I pitched an interesting and unique angle. (G)

If you are not familiar with writing press releases, go to your public library and check out a book on writing news releases, or use the internet for further instruction.

Submitting to television stations is not that much different. Sending your news release along with your book(s) to the host of a morning news segment may very well get you on television.

I have been interviewed for a morning show in Portland, Oregon and featured in an education segment in El Paso, Texas. (R)

Mailings cost more money (price of postage as well as postcards or flyers), but don't end up in a spam folder (a place where your email software sends incoming emails it believes are unsolicited). If your mailing is well laid out, on good paper, and catches the attention of the receiver, it may be kept or filed for future reference, or of course, it could end up in the garbage can. You never know.

I depend on mailings that I participate in with a group of other presenters/performers. I pay to be included and the mailings are done four times a year to schools and libraries. Most of the work I get comes from mailings.(G)

There are also companies that do mailings to bookstores and libraries. These mailings will not generate speaking engagements directly, but will make establishments aware of the title and the author.

Phone calls can be instrumental in identifying contact persons. You may be looking for the name of the school librarian or the children's librarian at a public library. Calling for this information will save you from addressing your mailings or communications to the wrong individual. If you feel comfortable making your sales pitch on the phone, go for it. Have your pitch practiced so you don't run on and on. After all, they are busy also.

I personally don't make phone calls. When I have already been hired and I am presenting, I make known that I am available for future presentations. I try to connect and promote interest in what I have written at my presentation. (G)

Conferences are one of the options you could pursue to promote yourself. PTA conferences, teacher conferences, and library showcases are a few of the available places to set up a booth, present your book(s), handout your promotional materials, and make one-on-one connections with people who can facilitate your being hired. Perseverance, consistency, and constant promotion will be the best road. Conference tables/booths vary in price from $50.00 to over $1000.00

Speaker organizations are another option. There are websites that charge a large sum of money to list you as an author willing to present. Your photograph, books, location, and your fees are posted. Find the ones you can afford and see if they are a right fit for you.

I am not with a speaker's bureau because as a children's performer/author, I pass out my flyers and catalogs at my shows to an audience that is already coming to see me. Most of my sales come from an audience who has seen me in person. (G)

I, on the other hand, have opted to list with a speaker agent who, for a yearly fee, actively promotes my speaking ser-

vices(R)

Speaking contracts should include: your name/your company name, the name of the school/library, the dates, time, location of presentation, the amount to be paid, the date payment is expected (within 30 days of presentation), arrangements to be made in case of cancellation by either party, signature lines for both parties.

||||||||||||||||||||||||||||||||||||||||||||||||||||||||||||||||||||||||||||||||||||||||||||||||||||||||||||||||||||||||||||||||

Sample Speaker Agreement:

This agreement is made and entered into this date, by and between <u>Client Name</u> and <u>Speaker Name</u>. Speaker agrees to prepare and present the following program(s) at <u>   Location with address   </u> on<u>   Day   </u> of event <u> , Date </u>at <u> Time </u>. <u>Client Name </u> will pay <u>Speaker Name </u> an honorarium in the amount of <u> $0000 </u>issued at the conculsion of Speaker's presentation. If for any reason, Speaker is delayed or cannot appear, Speaker will promptly notify Client to arrange a mutually agreeable change of date and/or a substitute Speaker. Any benefits, deposits, and/or advance reimbursements under this agreement shall be transferred to the substitute Speaker, if any. If a change of date of substitute Speaker cannot be mutually agreed upon, Client and Speaker agree that this agreement is cancelled and that Speaker shall refund any deposits and/or advance reimbursements received from Client.

Authorized Signatures:

By: _____ Date: _____
Tax ID/SSN: _____
Client: _____
Speaker: _____

||||||||||||||||||||||||||||||||||||||||||||||||||||||||||||||||||||||||||||||||||||||||||||||||||||||||||||||||||||||||||||||||

Sample Invoice:

Ramona Winner
Tax ID
BRAINSTORM 3000
P.O. Box 80513
Goleta, CA 93118

Invoice

Date	Invoice No.
11/29/15	594

Bill To:
ABC School
123 Country Lane
Everywhere, USA 93312

Ship To

P.O. Number	Terms	Rep	Ship Date	Ship Via	FOB	Project
	Net 30		11/29/15			

Item	Description	Quantity	Price Each	Amount
School Presentation	Assemblies	3		0.00
	Three school assemblies beginning at 8:00 a.m. on February 20, 2017 at at 123 Country Lane, Everywhere USA			
	Terms are 30 days net, but you can request payment upon completion of assemblies.			0.00

Thank you for your business!

	Total	$0.00

Follow through on the work that you have done. You sent materials to the school, now call and make sure they received them. A few days before your presentation, call and confirm that they are expecting you.

When you get a booking, tell everyone! Email the information to your friends and acquaintances, send it out to the newspaper calendar where you will be presenting, put it on on-line calendars, get it out on social media: Facebook, Linkedin, Twitter, and the like. If you have no idea what those are, find a friend who does who can help you ease into the current way of staying in touch.

As authors we want to ensure our books are seen so they have an opportunity to be bought. However, it works against us if we change our relationships with people on line just to make a sales pitch.

Robert Hunter IV explained, "Too many people are still using social media platforms as nothing more than a way to push marketing messages into the faces of their customers. This is strange to me because if they were face-to-face with their customers I'm sure they would never act that way."

No One Knows Who You Are: Make Some Noise

There are countless creative ways to making yourself known. One of the less difficult is to put together a press packet of yourself including information about your book(s), a photo and biography, and how you can be contacted. Write a letter to a school principal (include your press packet) explaining that you would like to present your book(s), **free of charge**, to a particular student body audience. Explain there will be no charge, but that you would like to send out pre-order book fliers and pass out flyers at the event. Once they agree, book the date, confirm, drop off flyers, establish your contact, and give them your best. You may or may not get orders. Hurray if you do! The school might buy a copy of your book(s) for its library. If you enjoyed the experience, try it at another school, a local bookstore, or a recreation center.

Wayne Dyer, a motivational speaker and internationally renowned author of over 40 books on self-development, traveled the United States in a station wagon full of his first book (as the story goes). He stopped off at bookstores along the way, promoting his book and selling as he went. Dyer set up media interviews and, through tireless efforts, his book *Your Erroneous Zones* reached the best-seller list.

Your job as an author does not end when your book is published. What path will you choose to share it with the world?

Attitude and Gratitude

Be cheerful, friendly, and kind at all times while at your venue. The teacher or librarian who facilitated your visit has her own job, her own life, and her own worries. That individual's job does not require him/her to coddle you and commiserate with whatever challenges you had that day or have been having in your life. Do not burden him/her with anything.

Your sole function on visiting the school is to share your book(s), bring joy to the children, inspire children to read, and to make the experience a positive one.

If you were stuck in a hailstorm while an earthquake was taking place, and you had to change a flat tire **and** your clothes in the trunk of your car, no one wants to hear that. Take your frustrations home and share them with your friends and family, your journal or your guru, not at the school.

They will remember you as the author who did not complain even though you could not find a parking space in the school lot. They will remember you as someone who was soaking wet in the rain but still told a story with a good, cheerful attitude. That is your legacy; that is what will allow a recommendation to take place. If you are fuming, you should not be manifesting it out in the physical world on that school campus.

The success of your book is in your hands. The tools provided here for you have been tried and have worked. Implement the ones you are most comfortable with and try others you know you could master.

Don't give up, presevere. Like in all sales, it is a numbers game. We would not have enjoyed the light bulb when we did, had the inventor, Thomas Edison, given up on his over 2998 different designs!

About the Authors of This Book

Ramona Moreno Winner has been a publisher and author of children's bilingual/multicultural books since 1996. A world traveler, Ramona has visited Japan, Korea, China, Africa, India, South America, Malaysia, Vietnam, Mexico, Canada, Seychelles, Portugal, and Cuba. Her award winning books and her presentations reflect her experiences in her travels.

Born and raised in Arizona, Ramona is a third generation Mexican who can readily remember not being accepted for her cultural background. Not ever feeling she belonged, Ramona found herself straddling two cultures. Today, her mission is to write books that make her readers realize they we are more similar than different.

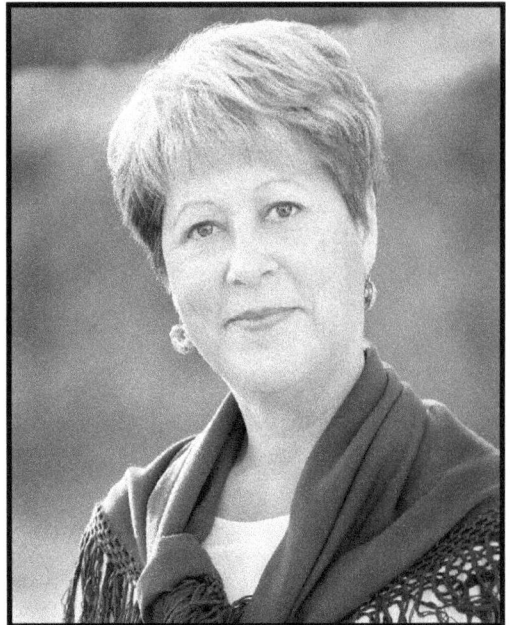

Although Ramona is not fluent in Spanish, she does converse and present in both English and Spanish. Ramona loves to hike, read books, loves trivia, and appreciates history. Mostly, Ramona loves to laugh!

Certified by the National Alliance on Mental Illness, Ramona is equipped to teach the Family to Family 12 week course for family members, caregivers, and friends of individuals living with mental illness. She is a volunteer at the local Mental Wellness Center, and supports her own son as he navigates life with a diagnosis of schizophrenia.

You can learn more about Ramona by visiting her websites: www.brainstorm3000.com featuring Ramona's books and school assemblies, and www.plantsoa.us for Ramona's diversity workshops for eductors.

Georgette Baker established her own company, Cantemos, and produces a line of children's bilingual books and music. Baker is a certified teacher, speaker of five languages, and a world-traveling performer. Georgette is author of more than 32 bilingual books and CD's for children. She is also a singer, storyteller, educator, mother, and grandmother.

Georgette has mastered the art of storytelling combining words with interactive songs she plays on her guitar. Georgette was born in Aruba, grew up in Venezuela, and spent several years in Ecuador and Greece. Baker writes books about places she loves. All her books and her bilingual CD's of traditional songs from Mexico and South America are a result of her multicultural experiences.

To learn more about Georgette, visit her website at www.simplespanishsongs.com. You can contact Georgette at bakergeorgette@yahoo.com

www.ingramcontent.com/pod-product-compliance
Lightning Source LLC
Chambersburg PA
CBHW060646280326
41933CB00012B/2179